bill
martin
books

Bill Martin Jr, Ph.D., has devoted his life to the education of young children. Bill Martin Books reflect his philosophy: that children's imaginations are opened up through the play of language, the imagery of illustration, and the permanent joy of reading books.

Henry Holt and Company, Inc., *Publishers since 1866,*
115 West 18th Street, New York, New York 10011.
Henry Holt is a registered trademark of
Henry Holt and Company, Inc.

Library of Congress Cataloging-in-Publication Data
Merriam, Eve. Bam, bam, bam / by Eve Merriam; illustrated by
Dan Yaccarino. "A Bill Martin book." Summary: In this noisy
poem, a wrecking ball demolishes old houses and stores to make
way for a skyscraper.   1. Wrecking—Juvenile poetry.
2. Children's poetry, American.   [1. Wrecking—Poetry.
2. American poetry.]   I. Yaccarino, Dan, ill.   II. Title.
PS3525.E639B25   1995   811 .54—dc20   94-20300
The paintings for this book were done with alkyds on bristol paper.
ISBN 0-8050-3527-3   First Edition—1995
Printed in the United States of America on acid-free paper. ∞
1 3 5 7 9 10 8 6 4 2

3 1235 01003 2998

A Bill Martin
Book
Henry Holt
and Company
New York

BAM
BAM
BAM

Written by
Eve Merriam

illustrated by
Dan Yaccarino

Workmen are covered with white dust like snow.

Oh, come see the great demolition show!

SLAM, SLAM, SLAM,

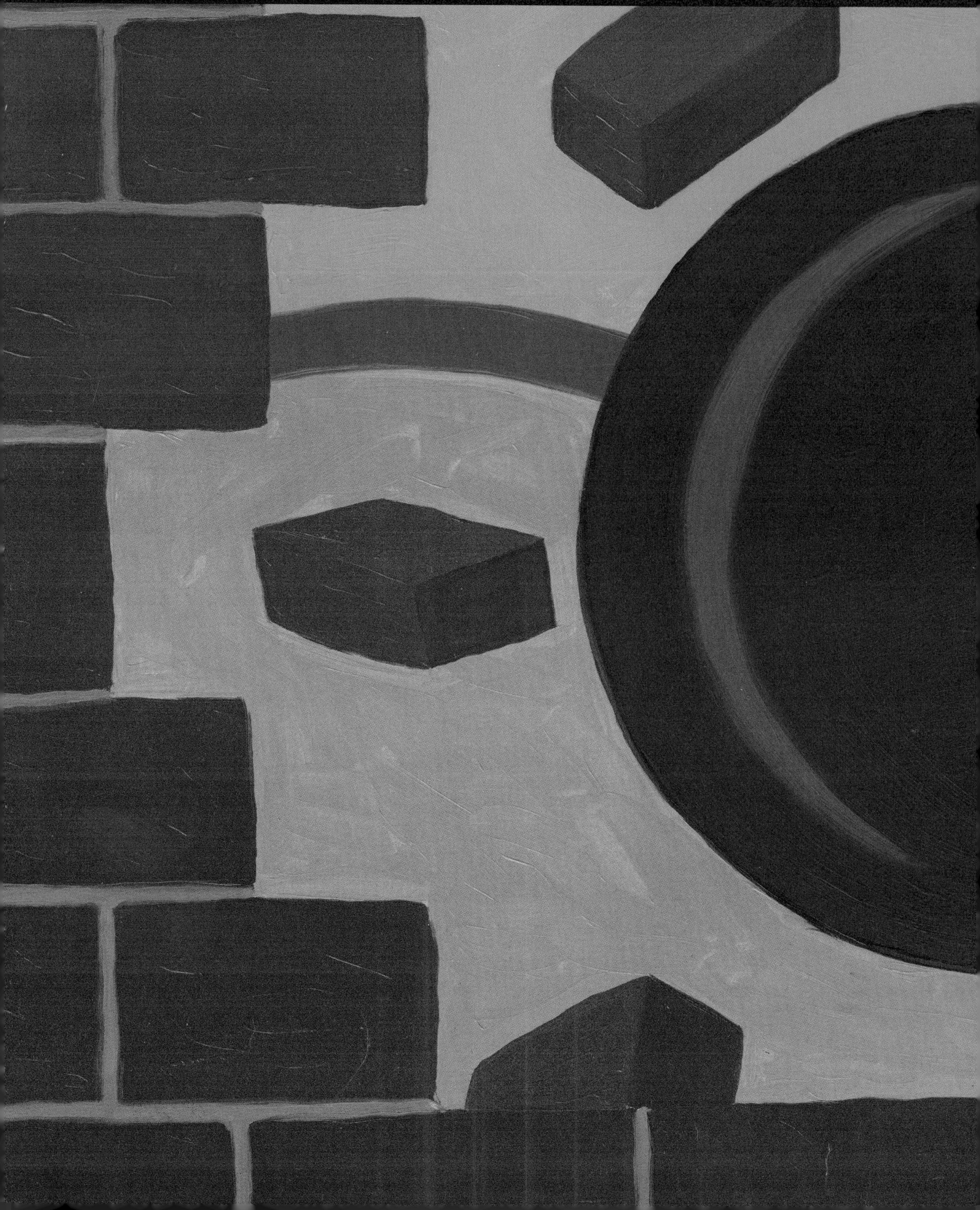

goes the steel wrecking-ball,

BAM, BAM, BAM,

against a stone wall.

It's raining bricks and wood

in my neighborhood.

Down go the houses,

down go the stores,

CRASH goes a chimney,

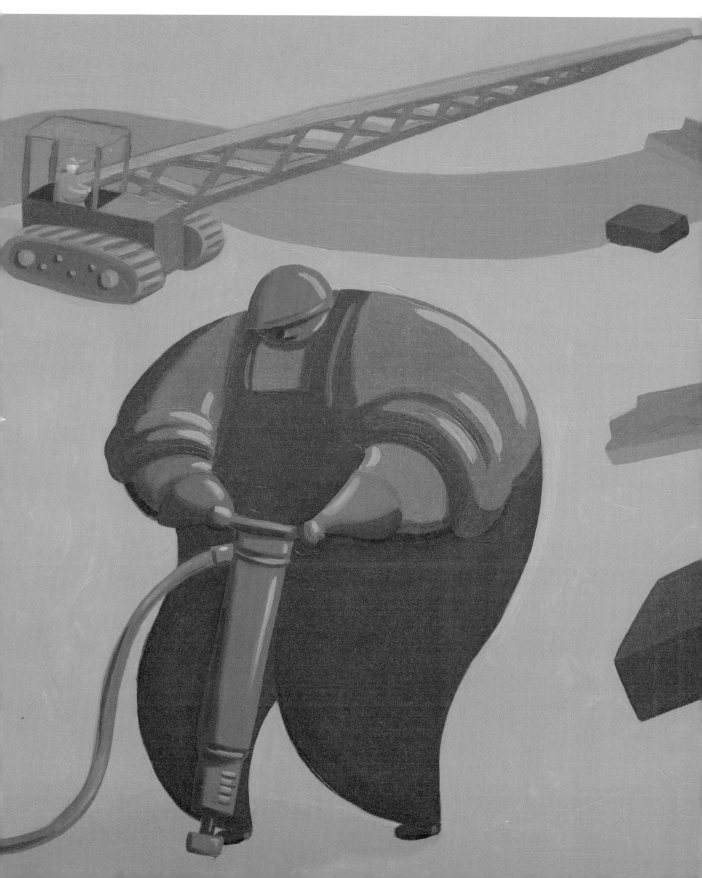

POW goes a hall,

ZOWIE goes a doorway,

ZAM goes a wall.

SLAM, SLAM, SLAM,

BAM, BAM, BAM,

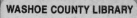

changing it all.